CW00420878

Nailed It!
A Handbook for Nail Technicians

Table of Contents

Nailed It!
A Handbook for Nail Technicians

Nailed It!
A Handbook for Nail Technicians

Nailed It!
A Handbook for Nail Technicians

Nailed It!
A Handbook for Nail Technicians

Thank You & Dedication

To every aspiring beauty professional reading this,

Thank you for embarking on this transformative journey with me. This book is a manifestation of love, passion, and an unwavering dedication to the beauty industry. It aims to guide you meticulously, step-by-step, item by item, leaving no stone unturned.

This book is wholeheartedly dedicated to everyone who seeks a comprehensive checklist to hone their skills and services. If you're passionate about knowledge and driven to deliver unparalleled services, consider this guide as my commitment to your growth and success.

The Louisville Beauty Academy stands as a beacon of hope, ambition, and perseverance. It was envisioned and founded as a sanctuary where every beauty enthusiast, irrespective of their background, can find solace and purpose. For every immigrant, every new American navigating the challenges of language and cultural assimilation, for every individual feeling marginalized or overwhelmed, I want you to know that this academy was crafted with you at its heart. As a Vietnamese immigrant, I, Di Tran, have traversed this journey. I've embraced the challenges, felt the isolation, yet emerged resilient.

I must extend my deepest gratitude to all the staff and instructors of Di Tran Enterprise and Louisville Beauty Academy. Without your unwavering dedication and commitment, our mission wouldn't be the thriving reality it is today. You've been instrumental in elevating and transforming thousands of lives, and the ripple effect of our collective endeavors will continue to touch many more souls in the years to come.

Our academy is more than just a place of learning; it's a mission to serve those segments of the community that often remain in the shadows—the elderly, the differently-abled, and all those in between. We aim to not just mold beauty professionals, but compassionate individuals who recognize the value of serving everyone with love and respect.

Beyond the art of beauty lies a promising business landscape. Every beauty professional deserves the opportunity to prosper, provide for their family, and leave an indelible mark in the industry.

Nailed It!
A Handbook for Nail Technicians

This book embodies that belief. It represents a journey—one of dreams, tenacity, and the undying spirit of the beauty sector. As you flip through these pages, I invite you to join us in this quest, and together, we'll craft beauty, one nail, one strand, one face at a time.

With profound gratitude and dedication,

Di Tran

Co-Founder and CEO of Louisville Beauty Academy

Nailed It!
A Handbook for Nail Technicians

Chapter 1: Manicures

Pre-Service Setup:

- Disinfect all tools with EPA-approved solutions – nail files, clippers, cuticle pushers, tweezers, etc.
- Wash hands thoroughly with soap and water
- Fill finger bowl with warm water and gentle soap
- Set out towels, cotton rounds, orangewood sticks, polish remover, nail buffers, lotions
- Select base coat, color polish and top coat
- Cover work surface with clean paper/towels

Client Consultation:

- Greet client and introduce yourself
- Review client intake form and discuss desired services
- Assess the condition of the client's nails and skin
- Ask about any allergies or sensitivities
- Explain the manicure process and what to expect

Nailed It!
A Handbook for Nail Technicians

Prep Client's Nails:
- Have client wash their hands with soap and water and dry thoroughly
- Gently push back cuticles with a cuticle pusher/orangewood stick as needed – do not cut cuticles
- File nails to desired shape using gentle, even strokes
- Soak nails in finger bowl for 5-10 minutes to soften cuticles and nails

Cleanse Nails:
- Use nail brush and soap to gently scrub under free edge and around nails
- Rinse soap off fully with clean water
- Dry hands and nails thoroughly with a clean towel

Massage:
- Apply lotion/cream and massage client's hands and arms
- Soft, gentle kneading motions
- Avoid bony prominences like wrist bones
- Massage each finger as well

Polishing:
- Use dehydrator/primer if needed for polish adhesion

Nailed It!
A Handbook for Nail Technicians

- Apply base coat and let dry fully
- Apply 2 coats of selected polish and let dry between coats
- Apply top coat for shine and protection
- Use LED light to cure polish if desired

Final Steps:

- Use cuticle oil to hydrate nails and skin
- Perform final check of manicure result
- Provide post-care instructions
- Share recommendations for maintenance

Clean Up:

- Properly dispose of any soiled cotton, tissues etc.
- Remove used polish bottles and replace caps tightly
- Disinfect all tools fully
- Wash hands again after taking off gloves
- Wipe down table and chair with disinfectant

Chapter 2: Pedicures

Pre-Service Setup:

- Clean and disinfect pedicure chair and foot basin
- Fill basin with warm water and gently cleansing soap
- Disinfect all tools – foot files, nail clippers, cuticle pushers etc.
- Wash hands thoroughly and put on gloves
- Set out towels, exfoliant scrub, lotions, cuticle oil
- Select base coat, color polish and top coat

Client Consultation:

- Greet client and have them complete intake form
- Discuss medical history and medications
- Assess condition of feet and nails, check for infections or contraindications
- Explain service process and what to expect

Prep Client's Feet:

- Have client wash feet with soap and water

Nailed It!
A Handbook for Nail Technicians

- Remove old polish gently with remover
- Soak feet in basin for 5-10 minutes
- Use foot file to gently remove calluses if needed
- Push back cuticles as needed with orangewood stick

Cleanse Feet:

- Wash feet thoroughly with soap, water and nail brush
- Use exfoliant scrub on soles and heels in circular motions
- Rinse away all soap residue and dry feet well

Massage:

- Apply massage oil/lotion and work into feet and legs
- Knead muscles from toes to knees using light pressure
- Pay special attention to arch and heel

Polishing:

- Use primer if needed to help polish adhere
- Apply base coat and let dry fully
- Apply 2 coats of selected polish, drying between coats

Nailed It!
A Handbook for Nail Technicians

- Apply top coat for protection and shine
- Use LED lamp to cure polish if desired

Final Steps:

- Apply cuticle oil to hydrate nail beds
- Do final check of pedicure result
- Provide post-care instructions
- Share tips for continued foot health

Clean Up:

- Assist client in standing up slowly and safely
- Provide slippers/socks to wear walking out
- Properly dispose of soiled materials
- Drain, clean and fully disinfect pedicure basin
- Disinfect all tools and implements
- Wash hands after taking off gloves
- Wipe down chair, station and floor with disinfectant

Chapter 3: Acrylic/Gel Nails

Pre-Service Setup:

- Disinfect work surface and chair/stool
- Wash hands thoroughly and prepare gloves
- Select tips and adhesive based on client's nails
- Set out acrylic/gel products and sculpting tools
- Have primer, dehydrator, nail files, buffers nearby
- Turn on ventilation system if available

Consultation:

- Review client's intake form
- Discuss desired nail shape and length
- Assess natural nails for conditions or contraindications
- Explain process for applying, filling, and removing acrylic/gel
- Discuss maintenance needs

Prep Natural Nails:

- Gently push back and trim cuticles if needed
- Use dehydrator/primer to prep nails for tips
- Select proper nail tip size and custom fit to nail

Nailed It!
A Handbook for Nail Technicians

- Glue on tips securely using nail adhesive

Shape and Apply Product:
- Use file to shape and blend tip with natural nail edge
- Apply new primer coat if needed
- Apply acrylic/gel product over nail following manufacturer instructions
- Sculpt and form product into desired nail shape
- Let set fully until hardened

Finish and Shape:
- Use nail file to refine shape and smooth surface
- Buff nails for natural shine and radiance
- Use nail cleanser/dehydrator to remove oil and dust

Final Steps:
- Massage nails and cuticles with oil
- Educate on fill schedule based on growth
- Share tips for maintenance and removal
- Provide client home care instructions

Clean Up:
- Properly dispose of used materials

Nailed It!
A Handbook for Nail Technicians

- Carefully remove and disinfect all sculpting tools
- Fully clean and disinfect work station
- Remove gloves and thoroughly wash hands

Chapter 4: Nail Art

Pre-Service Setup:

- Disinfect work surface and tools
- Select base polishes and art materials
- Set out brushes, dotting tools, embellishments
- Have top coat, drying lamps, nail cleanser available
- Prepare camera for design inspiration

Client Consultation:

- Discuss client's preferences for design, colors, theme
- Show portfolio samples or look at options online together
- Explain process and timeline to client
- Agree on final design plan

Prep Nails:

- Start with cleaned, filed, healthy nails
- Apply base coat and let dry fully
- Apply background color polish evenly and let dry

Create Design:

- Follow agreed upon design plan
- Use variety of polish colors to paint on main design

Nailed It!
A Handbook for Nail Technicians

- Let polish dry fully between layers and details
- Affix embellishments like glitter, foils or gems if desired

Finish Art:

- Apply fast-drying top coat to seal in design
- Use LED lamp to cure layers and set embellishments
- Suggest maintenance tips to keep art looking fresh

Final Steps:

- Massage in cuticle oil around nail beds
- Provide instructions for safe removal
- Share tips for preserving manicure

Clean Up:

- Properly dispose of used materials
- Sanitize all reusable tools and brushes
- Replace polishes and art supplies
- Disinfect work area and chair/stool
- Wash hands thoroughly after removing gloves

Nailed It!
A Handbook for Nail Technicians

Nail Art Techniques

- Striping - Using a striping brush and colored polish to create straight, diagonal or wavy lines.
- Dots - Using a dotting tool dipped in polish to create different size dots across the nail.
- Marbling - Dropping various colors into water and swiping nails through to create a marbled effect.
- Ombre - Gradually blending two or more shades of polish from light to dark.
- Stamping - Using a metal plate and stamper to transfer designs onto the nail.
- Decals - Applying pre-made polish stickers or decals onto the nail surface.
- Encapsulation - Suspending glitters, sequins or other embellishments under a layer of top coat.
- Freehand - Using a steady hand to paint intricate designs directly onto nails.

Nail Art Examples:

- Polka dots
- Chevron or zig zag patterns
- Animal print

Nailed It!
A Handbook for Nail Technicians

- Florals and botanical designs
- Geometric shapes and lines
- Galaxy or cosmic colors
- Holiday themes like hearts, shamrocks, snowflakes etc.
- French tip ombre
- glitter ombre
- Jewel, bead or rhinestone encrusted
- Painted scenic landscapes

Striping:

- Start with a base color on all nails and let dry completely.
- Using a striping brush, dip into a contrasting polish color.
- Holding the brush steady, paint on straight lines vertically, diagonally, or horizontally across the nail.
- You can connect the lines into chevron patterns or leave them single.
- Let dry before moving on to any additional designs.

Stamping:

- Apply base coat and let dry. Paint nails in a single color.
- Choose a stamping plate design and scrape excess polish off the surface.
- Roll stamper over design to transfer image.

Nailed It!
A Handbook for Nail Technicians

- Line stamper up on nail and press down firmly to imprint design.
- Repeat across all nails using different areas of plate.
- Finish with a fast-drying top coat to seal.

Ombre:

- Paint nails in a light base color and let fully dry.
- Using makeup sponges, dab on your chosen darker colors higher up on the nail bed.
- While polish is still wet, use downward strokes to softly blend and fade the colors into the base.
- Work quickly before polish dries. Continue blending for a smooth gradient.
- Apply glossy top coat to lock in the ombre effect.

Chapter 5: Customer Service and Client Relations

Greeting Clients:

- Smile warmly and make eye contact when clients enter your salon space.
- Greet them right away with an enthusiastic "Hello!" or "Good morning/afternoon."
- Use their name if known and say "It's nice to see you again [name]!"
- For new clients, introduce yourself and offer a handshake. "Hi, I'm [your name], it's nice to meet you."

Interacting During Service:

- Maintain a positive attitude and cheerful demeanor throughout the entire service.
- Give your undivided attention to the client in front of you.
- Make friendly small talk and ask questions to learn more about them.
- Listen attentively when clients are speaking. Provide words of encouragement.
- Explain each step before you do it and keep them informed of timing.
- Check in regularly on comfort and satisfaction.

Nailed It!
A Handbook for Nail Technicians

Finishing the Service:
- Thank clients sincerely for choosing your services.
- Ask if they are pleased with the final result. Offer to make any adjustments.
- Provide specific compliments on their new look.
- Remind them of booking their next appointment.
- Walk them to the reception desk and bid them a warm goodbye.

Going the Extra Mile:
- Use client's name frequently. Address them as "Ma'am" or "Sir."
- Offer refreshments like water, coffee or tea during longer services.
- Accommodate special requests or modifications whenever possible.
- Give an occasional free extra like nail art or polish touch up.
- Send a thank you text or email after the service.

Handling Busy Times:
- If running behind schedule, apologize sincerely to clients for the wait.
- Offer a small gift like a bottle of polish or cuticle oil as an apology.

Nailed It!
A Handbook for Nail Technicians

- Explain the reason for the delay and keep them updated on timing.
- Thank them for their patience and understanding.
- Consider offering a discount or free express service next visit.

Addressing Complaints:

- Listen carefully and don't interrupt if a client complains.
- Express empathy and apologize that they had a negative experience.
- Ask questions to fully understand the issue from their perspective.
- Do not blame others or make excuses. Take responsibility.
- Come up with potential solutions to remedy the situation.
- Thank them for taking the time to share feedback.
- Follow up after the service to check satisfaction.

Interacting with Different Clients:

- Be patient with elderly clients and allow extra time as needed.
- Chat with shy clients to help them feel comfortable.
- Gauge conversations based on client cues and don't pry.

Nailed It!
A Handbook for Nail Technicians

- Adjust pressure during massages according to client response.
- Be prepared to accommodate those with physical limitations.
- Keep interactions kid-friendly with young children as clients.

Chapter 6: Cashier Best Practices

Processing Payment:

- Give the total due in a friendly, clear manner and make eye contact.
- Allow clients time to retrieve their payment method. Don't rush them.
- Keep the transaction area neat and have a pen ready.
- Inform clients of payment options like cash, credit, gift cards, etc.
- Thank each client after processing payment.
- Provide a detailed receipt with your name, service details, and salon info.

Soliciting Feedback:

- Ask if the client is satisfied with their service that day.
- Inquire if there is any feedback they'd like to share with management.
- Have paper surveys or tablets ready to capture reviews.
- Let them know their feedback is appreciated and helps improve service.
- Follow up each service by sending a text or email linking to your online review platform.

Nailed It!
A Handbook for Nail Technicians

- Periodically offer incentives like discounts for leaving reviews.
- Respond professionally to any online reviews whether good or bad.

Additional Tips:

- Accurately answer questions about service and pricing.
- Know current promotions or deals to inform clients.
- Upsell retail products like nail polish, files, lotions etc.
- Be knowledgeable about appointments and booking.
- Maintain client confidentiality and discretion.

Handling Returns & Exchanges:

- Apologize and thank the client for bringing the item they wish to return or exchange.
- Do not ask why or make them feel guilty. Simply comply with your salon's policy.
- Examine merchandise and proof of purchase if needed.
- Offer options like a full refund, exchange for a different product, or in-store credit.

Nailed It!
A Handbook for Nail Technicians

- Let manager handle any returns without a receipt or that seem suspicious.
- Thank the client for understanding and allow them to take their time selecting a replacement item if exchanging.

Promoting Retail:

- Keep displays of retail products fully stocked and neatly presented.
- Mention relevant items clients may be interested in purchasing.
- For example, recommend cuticle oil after a manicure.
- Share details on newest collections or products. Offer samples.
- Have promotional offers like discounts or free samples available at checkout.
- Bundle items together or create gift sets for easy gifting.

Handling Client Information:

- Keep client records organized and confidential.
- Verify identity before providing personal information.
- Obtain permission before taking or posting photos.

Nailed It!
A Handbook for Nail Technicians

- Be mindful of phone conversations - do not disclose details loudly.
- Keep computer screens with client data out of public view.
- Securely dispose of client intake forms or notes containing sensitive information.

Managing Inventory:

- Take note of popular items selling out quickly to identify bestsellers.
- Track inventory levels to know when to reorder retail products or salon supplies.
- Organize storage areas and arrange products neatly by category.
- Perform regular inventory checks and audits to watch for discrepancies.
- Protect assets by securing products, cash, equipment in locked areas.
- Report any damaged or expired goods.

Handling Payroll:

- Verify employee hours and double check payroll for accuracy.
- Maintain payroll payment records and documentation.
- Distribute pay stubs in a discrete and timely manner.

Nailed It!
A Handbook for Nail Technicians

- Withhold proper taxes and deductions for each employee per regulations.
- Process commission payouts for service providers following salon guidelines.
- Provide year-end tax statements.

Cash Register Safety:

- Keep cash drawers closed when not actively in use.
- Regularly drop large bills from the drawer into a safe.
- Never leave the register unattended or let unauthorized staff use it.
- Count and reconcile the cash/sales at the start and end of each shift.
- Balance the books and report any discrepancies right away.
- Change passcodes periodically and limit access to managers only.

Greeting Clients:

- Welcome clients to the salon and direct them where to wait/go.
- Offer a warm greeting regardless of how busy you are.
- Introduce yourself by name and ask if you can help find their stylist.

Nailed It!
A Handbook for Nail Technicians

Answering Phone Calls:

- Answer calls in a friendly and professional manner. State the salon name.
- Have booking information available to help schedule appointments.
- Take messages for stylists/technicians who are with clients.
- Return voicemails and unanswered calls promptly.

Managing Wait Times:

- Apologize if walk-in clients must wait to be seen. Provide an estimated time.
- Offer a beverage or magazine while they wait.
- Give status updates to waiting clients if possible.
- Thank them sincerely for their patience.

Resolving Issues:

- Listen fully if a client has a complaint or problem. Show empathy.
- Take responsibility, remain calm, and avoid blame.
- Collaborate with managers and staff to formulate a fair solution.

- Follow up to ensure the issue was resolved properly.

Maintaining Work Area:

- Keep desk and cash wrap free of clutter.
- Frequently sanitize work surfaces.
- Restock forms, business cards, pens, mints etc. when low.
- Advise manager when office supplies are running out.

Processing Appointments:

- Verify available times and confirm bookings in the scheduler or software system.
- Double check client name, contact information, and service details.
- Provide appointment date, time, location, and stylist name.
- Remind clients to arrive 10-15 mins early for check-in.
- Offer booking incentives like discounts on future services.

Cross-Training:

- Shadow other roles like receptionists to learn salon workflow.
- Study service menus and prices to be able to answer common questions.

Nailed It!
A Handbook for Nail Technicians

- Refresh knowledge of promotions, membership programs, or events.
- Practice booking mock appointments in the scheduler.
- Learn to balance the cash drawer and perform closing duties.

Continuing Education:

- Attend manufacturer trainings on new products carried.
- Complete online courses on salon software or other relevant topics.
- Read beauty industry blogs, magazines, books to stay updated.
- Participate in local community events and classes when possible.
- Join professional associations to network and develop skills.

Teamwork:

- Collaborate with desk staff to provide excellent customer experiences.
- Communicate openly with managers regarding goals and issues.
- Offer assistance to technicians/stylists when not busy.
- Provide guidance and training to new hires as needed.

Opening/Closing Procedures

Nailed It!
A Handbook for Nail Technicians

- Arrive early before opening to prep workstation, organize cash drawer, brew coffee.
- Power on computer, printer, credit card machine and test connections.
- Review appointment book and prep client files for the day.
- At closing, reconcile credit card receipts and cash drawer totals.
- Process end-of-day reporting and payments.
- Restock retail displays, clean up reception area.
- Secure salon entrance, arm security system.

Promoting Services

- Familiarize yourself with all service offerings to explain to clients.
- Make recommendations based on client hair/nail type and needs.
- Cross-sell add-on services like deep conditioning or paraffin dips.
- Share current promotions for retail items or service specials.
- Hand out business cards and encourage online reviews/referrals.

Nailed It!
A Handbook for Nail Technicians

Managing Supplies

- Take inventory of sundry items and order more when stock is low.
- Check treatment rooms have enough towels, robes, slippers etc.
- Organize storage closets and request items to be reordered.
- Ensure coffee stations, water dispensers are continually stocked.
- Advise manager on any equipment issues needing repair.

Managing Gift Cards:

- Keep gift card inventory organized and track serial numbers.
- Clearly explain gift card policies like expiration dates and blackout periods.
- Allow gift card recipients to book services directly instead of purchaser.
- Process gift cards as payment and handle balances carefully.
- Replace lost, stolen or damaged cards per your policies.
- Regularly check state laws regarding unused gift card liabilities.

Handling Tips:

- Count and secure tip money discreetly in front of client.

Nailed It!
A Handbook for Nail Technicians

- Maintain tip logs and have technicians verify their totals.
- Divide and distribute tips accurately based on policies.
- Track tip earnings for tax purposes.
- Politely decline tips as a cashier if your employer does not allow it.

Salon Ambiance:

- Keep noise levels, music, and lighting comfortable in reception area.
- Maintain tidy, organized, and clutter-free front desk space.
- Display updated service menus and pricing.
- Have current product catalogs, magazines, or brochures on hand.
- Keep a pleasant fragrance in lobby with candles, oils, or sprays.

Staff Coordination:

- Communicate stylist availability to effectively book appointments.
- Verify appointments and client information with stylists/techs in advance.
- Notify staff of arrivals, late clients, or schedule changes promptly.

- Relay messages and important information between front/back of house.
- Offer to bring refreshments to stylists and technicians as needed throughout the day.
- Provide quick and courteous handling of any requests from service providers.

Salon Products Knowledge:

- Review product descriptions, key ingredients, pricing to advise clients.
- Learn which products complement various services.
- Get trained on proper product usage for hair types, nail care, skin etc.
- Attend manufacturer demo events to increase knowledge.
- Be able to articulate product features and benefits.
- Recommend appropriate home care regimens for each client.

Emergency Preparedness:

- Keep first aid and biohazard kits fully stocked.
- Know evacuation routes and emergency procedures.

Nailed It!
A Handbook for Nail Technicians

- Have emergency contacts and phone numbers on hand for quick access.
- Complete incident reports for any accidents or injuries on premises.
- Monitor severe weather and inform staff if threatening conditions arise.
- Take inventory of emergency supplies and restock as needed.

Customer Complaint Management:

- Listen empathetically and apologize sincerely when clients complain.
- Ask questions to fully understand the issues and don't assign blame.
- When possible, make reasonable accommodations to address the complaint.
- If unable to assist directly, explain that you will have a manager contact them.
- Report complaints promptly and document details in a log.
- Follow up with clients after resolving issue to ensure satisfaction.
- Analyze trends in feedback to improve operations.

Client Retention:

- Build rapport with regular clients and address them by name.

Nailed It!
A Handbook for Nail Technicians

- Record service and product preferences in client profiles.
- Proactively contact clients when they are due for a follow-up appointment.
- Send birthday, holiday cards or product samples to maintain relationships.
- Offer loyalty rewards or discounts on future services.
- Email occasional surveys to monitor satisfaction and improvement areas.

Salon Tours:

- Warmly greet prospective new clients and introduce yourself.
- Provide basic information about service offerings and tour the salon.
- Allow time to answer any questions they may have.
- Have brochures, business cards, and pricing information ready.
- Escort to appropriate staff member based on service of interest.
- Offer refreshments and make them feel comfortable in reception area.

Staff Training:

- Shadow experienced cashiers and learn salon systems.

Nailed It!
A Handbook for Nail Technicians

- Study service menus, pricing lists, promos to gain product knowledge.
- Practice booking and rescheduling appointments in the system.
- Learn proper cash handling procedures and sales reconciliation.
- Refresh customer service skills by role playing scenarios.
- Ask questions and clarify anything not fully understood.
- Review salon policies for returns, discounts, benefits, dress code.
- Complete any required safety or compliance training.

Workstation Organization:

- Keep supplies like pens, forms, calculators stocked and neatly arranged.
- Maintain organized files, magazines, menu cards within easy reach.
- Use desk organizers, trays to neatly store paperclips, rubber bands, etc.
- Minimize clutter and clear worksurface when not in active use.
- Place most frequently used items in top desk drawers for fast access.
- Keep computer desktop tidy and create useful shortcuts.

Nailed It!
A Handbook for Nail Technicians

Time Management:

- Create daily task lists and prioritize the most important responsibilities.
- Batch similar tasks together when possible to work efficiently.
- Allow enough time for each appointment when booking and reduce double-booking.
- Handle quick client requests like booking future appointments during down times.
- Minimize distractions and avoid multitasking when completing critical tasks.
- Stay organized and keep supplies within reach to avoid wasting time searching.
- Review schedule in advance and prepare for potentially busy times.

Stress Management:

- Take short breaks during the day to clear your head when needed.
- Avoid caffeine and other stimulants that can increase feelings of anxiety or tension.
- Use deep breathing techniques or step outside for a few minutes of fresh air.

Nailed It!
A Handbook for Nail Technicians

- Chat with coworkers briefly about non-work topics to decompress.
- Schedule lunch breaks and don't work through them. Refuel and recharge.
- Keep your workspace tidy and free of clutter to minimize environmental stressors.
- Talk to managers if you are feeling constantly stressed and overwhelmed.

Continuing Education:

- Take advantage of any advanced training courses offered on new products or services.
- Attend vendor workshops to learn about popular brands carried in the salon.
- Read industry magazines and blogs to stay up to date on the latest trends.
- Watch tutorials or webinars related to customer service and salon management.
- Sign up for relevant online courses to expand business knowledge and skills.
- Join local professional organizations to network and share best practices with peers.

Nailed It!
A Handbook for Nail Technicians

Personal Development:

- Set goals for growth and discuss development plans with managers.
- Identify strengths and weaknesses in your role through self-assessment.
- Welcome constructive feedback from team members and clients.
- Observe and learn from star performers in the salon.
- Keep growing your product knowledge and customer service skills.

Chapter Conclusion:

- Excellent cashiers are essential to the smooth operations and success of a salon.
- Mastering these best practices for payment processing, customer service, organization, and more allow cashiers to thrive and progress in their roles.

Conclusion

This comprehensive guide covers the core services and responsibilities within a professional nail salon. Mastering the techniques and best practices outlined in each chapter is essential for delivering an exceptional client experience.

The step-by-step procedures for manicures, pedicures, acrylics, nail art provide a roadmap for technicians to skillfully perform these popular nail services. Strict adherence to safety and sanitation protocols protects the health of both clients and staff.

Beyond technical skills, cultivating positive customer service and client relationships is paramount. Warm greetings, active listening, resolving issues, and exceeding expectations are hallmarks of a welcoming salon environment where clients feel pampered.

Behind the scenes, talented cashiers keep operations running smoothly. Organization, time management, product knowledge, and embracing technology allow them to juggle a demanding workload. Handling myriad tasks from appointment booking to inventory with a smile promotes a cohesive experience.

Continual learning is vital in this fast-paced industry. Whether participating in training courses, industry events, or reading on latest trends, growing your skills ensures clients receive the most current and innovative services.

In following the best practices outlined here, nail technicians and support staff alike develop the competence to thrive in their roles. A commitment to excellence, health and safety, and skill building allows salon team members to find meaning and enjoyment in this rewarding profession.

When executed with care and professionalism, salon services deliver far more than beautiful nails. The ritual pampering and renewal uplifts clients, providing a self-care experience that transcends the ordinary and rejuvenates spirit. This guide provides the blueprint to make that transformative experience a reality.

Let me know if you would like me to expand or modify the conclusion in any way. I can rework it to focus on different elements or add additional details. Please feel free to provide any other feedback as well!

THE END

THANK YOU

Printed in Great Britain
by Amazon